An Idea of Feathers

An Idea of Feathers

Poems

by Michael Hodges

BLUE SKETCH PRESS | PITTSBURGH

Contents

I.

III.

An Idea of Feathers

I

In the dream, every

Applebee's has been
abandoned. Children

play tag behind plywood
among the broken glass

and dethawed mozzarella
sticks. They evacuate

before the fires. The last
child to leave each

Applebee's says a prayer,
draws a circle in the dust

and ignites the Molotov.
The kids watch the fires

from the parking lot,
standing in the smoke

of charring babyback ribs

it's all so soothing

watching the before burn
itself to bones. Somewhen

a neon sign explodes
in every window. Menus

float hopefully skyward
like corporate-branded paper

cranes. Farewell again
to Friday's endless $9.99

appetizers and faux
homestyle fries, too bright

reconstituted potatoes,
powdered eggs scrambled

with cheese that will never
mold, farewell to walls

lined with plastic wood -
all melt as the children

watch, laughing, breath
bright in the falling air.

In a moment when we are made

to imagine new worlds, that we are present in
such a time, when we are made to imagine
ourselves living within, when the sky
seems again a limiting factor, in a moment
when such factors as time and the decay
of small droplets of water necessitate
reimagining the interior, beginning again
to consider decorating for functionality,
no soft surfaces, the air to be recycled
no less than once per - and the permitted
particle size to be no greater than - in such
a manner, when we are chosen to bare teeth
invisibly, to navigate the hallways of each
attention eyes-first and peel our hands
from anything soft or clinging to a moment
when we are meant to spawn new worlds
within our minds and live there, to exercise
such grand and infinitesimal gestures as -
or even the majesty and improbability of - in
such a time, when we are made an opening
mouth set behind a closed door, and all,
all made of such broad and tender imaginings -

I wake, and my left hand continues dreaming.

The night stays with it, in it, so it remains open
to all the stories the night would tell.
I thank the night for this gift, and my hand
for its openness. Each crawling pinprick of wrist
or palm or knuckle, a reminder that I slept,
that I became so unconscious of myself
if only for a few hours that I could fold my limbs
awkwardly and not think to unfold them.
I begin to feel my pulse again. The steady drum
of connection through every artery. This too,
worthy of thanks. This unpleasantry, the throb
of blood, the unkind warmth, the sweat
on my throat. This too a gift, to be so permeable
the warmth of me can disappear in water,
or through skin, or at any morning's unkind,
unpleasant, awkward, gentle start.

Notes on Walking

Seems so easy, the step - simply
unhinge, stay centered, weight
over the feet, fall forward, steady,

the catch, straighten, don't sissy,
don't hip too much - consider the knee,
how straightforward its world remains

unless something wobbles windless
from the stream, sail snagged
on a branch, brought crashing left,

or - alright, just track the straight line,
mark it with your eyes, make
a mark in the dust and fallow it

behind you, flay the sole
slowly against the soft rough
dust, or, perhaps you're barefoot,

stripped of rubber, one less
lift to catch too low, to lower

the bones but forget the nerves

and leave them to shudder raw
in the air, a whole needled mesh
of memory - when the foot buckles,

we say it has fallen asleep,
under the impression, perhaps,
perhaps it failed to alarm

as it should have, or, in its world
today the sun never rose,
never petaled, never cut-stem

and wilted through glass and oranged
the eyes through lids - regardless,
the step, given latitude to be thoughtless -

if you live in one thoughtless day,
the whole leg dreaming now
and every step a step in a dream

to run, and run, and never escape -
the road pursuing steady and slow
as a heartbeat, a hinge, a door, a jamb,

a wall, wandering through the whole house
and out, one step at a time, falling
forward and caught, tautened

like a tendon, already set to snap

its fingers and wake the sun,
who tingles up in a panic swallowing

yawns and all the still of night,
marrying stretch and escape,
untangling from bedclothes,

swinging a leg to the ground
and staggering unsteadily
from foot to footfall, finding

each step a stage for every center
to center on, around, past, and back
again for the next.

This dawn days the sky open

so unextravagantly it could be
a knife, the slim, sharp light
slicing through the soft flesh
of a tomato, a pitted olive,
an unwary hand, a heart
of palm. Every blade knows
she carries a leaf behind
her tongue. Today's clouds
bleed steppes of sepia, light
writing love letters to time
too tender to grace age
with slow fading, the same
language a slow-made meal
speaks to a friend's teeth.
A smile displays a mouth
full of dawning, each incisor
inscribing a reminder of fall,
of falling leaves, of the way
through sunrise to seasons
to season any meal the day
in all its unperfect light
and all its love requires.

Routine Orthostatic Hypotension

The gentle comedy   of rising. The ungainly
legs extending and   extending, all the hinges
dooring open. The arms   uncrooking from the lap,
who disappears   like I will someday.

I imagine standing   as a kind of death.
The world becomes a point   of light. A star
spinning in the infinite.   I am not unaware
of the laughter. Sound   catches in a belly

until it brings tears.   Until it tears open
a mouth and forces its way   out and through and into
the mourning world. When I stand   the world disappears.
For a moment there is nothing   but your face.

Laughing and then lined   with velvet
like a portrait of dead music.   Graveling all the new
standards. The right voice   for them. When the world
returns with my pulse   singing and my grip

on the handrail and all your concern   fading, then,
then too.

All Apologies

An anthropologist writes a history
of debt, claims we created a world
to track what was owed. If I owe

nothing, then there is nothing.
So too with my tongue. I know my words
by touch, by taste, by sound,

but more than all by what they signify
I owe so many things: the sky, who
is not silent, and knows nothing of debt,

but repays water for water endlessly;
my legs, who carry me even now;
now, who holds me in a flood of arms

I have not yet made my excuses
away from. So too with any debt.
So too with the words *I'm sorry.*

I say to them *I'm sorry the making
has become such a - I mean - the form,*

I'm sorry it's a - this morning,

I held them close like a cheap sweater.
I'm sorry - I wish they could feel how much
I am - how much they make I mean.

I say *I'm sorry I don't understand*
and then *I'm sorry for making excuses,*
it's just - I mean - not - I mean,

I'm not trying to - I mean,
I mean, I mean, like a kind
of invocation, as though if I mean

enough, I will, I mean, will be.
This morning I apologized
to the doorframe, for kicking it,

to my roommates, asleep a room away,
for the noise, though they slept -
still is a funny word, how it assumes

anything can stop apologizing
long enough to become stronger.
Sometimes I imagine a world

where everyone's gone except me
and my apologies. I think perhaps
even then, I'd find some tree,

or shrine, or stone, and say *I'm sorry,*

I'm sorry, try to summon back
my old failures, and, there, a world

I could hold close in its familiarity
until the scholars said *yes, yes,*
we're sorry, you could have known

this from the start, until the meaning
of all my meas culpa makes itself
a tongue that holds the sky together.

Mid-morning, I daydreamed of small vices

Set old habits on the bookshelf next
to every other wondrous thing as I sweated
and gasped to draw a metal bar closer.
I'm told if I force my heart to race
against itself, it will settle into a new
and more steady rhythm, that in the noise
of my tottering pulse it will find a place
it can call quiet, or peaceful, or slow.
The funniest thing about forgetting
must be the way it forgets to follow
any path. How it staggers from bramble
to stammer summoning small flames
from a hand's shudder. I remember
most mornings that it's after I cool
when I most want to breathe smoke.
I try to remember this is only a small
self-destruction, only a minor loss,
this rejection of desire, that though,
unlike the heart, the will does not grow
stronger by use, still, the small tears
will heal, will knit like any other wound.

still life with manic episode

& here (& we listen) in the top left
the floating light, dangling from the ceiling,
halogen bulb a swarm of fruit flies
filling the air beside my ear, the noisome thrall
of its distorted whine bright static
gray pervading everything. fastened
(& fascinated) with screws to the ceiling,
the mottled translucence of the fixture
(& we fixate on the disagreement between setting
& place) & here (& we are) the wall, set straight
down from a cobwebbed corner (i've been meaning,
been meaning to set the vacuum to it, to pull
each strand apart, but the absence is just so loud
& my housemates are asleep), mottled (also)
with dark gray specks (& each growing, & who am i
to tell anything not to become?) & meeting
the cabinet who i keep meaning to tell to become
organized, to develop their own voice
beyond the muddle of half-crushed tupperware
& the line of sugar ants i keep dissuading
(& who am i to stop this gray procession
from making its way across the featureless expanse?)

who i visit with bleach, splitting the cell walls
(as though i could become some abolitionist,
as though unmaking were a landscape
i could refashion into mine own image
(& isn't that fertile territory to plunder
(to strip & extract) & how many closings
must i navigate to become a full thought
or coherent (& here we consider the boundaries
of the sink, caulked (& isn't that a metaphor,
the closing with a thing meant to seal out water)
& the thin trail of damp across the countertop
where my cloth has left a trace, the strip of cloth
i'm about to discard into a reusable bag
(here, dangling split-handled from a door)
where all soiled things wait for the agitation
& the detergent, the rough chemical kiss
to misremember all history of usefulness & below the bag
the wood is splintered. once i stumbled & the impact
of fragile bone made more-fragile wood
a multiplicity (i haven't told the landlord
yet) & the bones were unharmed & bless that
unbreaking & the way it created a schism
& did not take it into itself (& i was not drunk
that morning, only clumsy, though my stumbling
did alarm those close to me) & still some fragments
linger there, scattered at the entrance
to another & perhaps more useful realm
& i have not made coffee yet, but will (with mine)
pour the beans from the faded bag
into a world of blades & follow them
with my eyes as they become something smaller

& made of surfaces (a thousand mirrors reflecting
my waking back upon itself) & pour a boiling
back across each surface i have made & take that
breaking back into myself (but now the kettle is cold,
the tarnish of the old steel a surface that reflects
nothing) & the water is unmoving in the pipes
& the kettle sits beside the burner judging me
for all my dream-ridden neglect, the handle
unwarmed, an unarmed trap, harmless,
a tripwire never raised from the ground.

On Narrative Coherence

I mean, the story's simple: the story's story
begins again every time the story begins
like night does, with something bright and painful
crawling beneath the horizon, the horizon's
teeth jagged with right angles and glass
and glassing the whole bright and painful landscape
painful like a painting a pointing a bringing back
the bringing bringing like morning does the light,
the light is simple, simples in straight lines
and lines up all the shadows and shadows all the ground
the ground lets be under, and under the light
the light isn't and isn't jagged, isn't jagged
like the noon before the evening wearies out the sharp.

I mean the dream's the same every time, time
peeling back the flesh and leaving the nerves
to nerve and hover before the bones, the bones
tendriled and fronded and coraled and bleached
and bleach scenting the anoxic sky, the sky
harboring like like like or like they lost their nerve
before they could say they loved anyone loved
by anyone bright, anyone else bright, anyone anyone

who could be and be being could be undone by
like the linear flow undoes the flow of light, light
said to set itself too far from star to star
to start with any kind of embrace and not embrace
the void first, the first following before following
anyone into any place that could be called warm.

I mean the waking's the part that parts the sea, sea
scent pervading the air, the air candled and candling
and candied with the salt, the salt setting and set
against the sky before the light can undo the light
the night provides, the night provides enough that enough
is a kind of kindness, a kindness to nerve and nothing
can nothing for long, it's too nervous to full, too full
for longing, too breathed to harbor in or harbor
anything uncharitable, I mean the story's simple:
simple the wake, wake the dead, dead the dream,
dream we woke and woke the sky and all the light
lighted on an on and on and kept going and we kept
the skyline lining the sky like an eye eyeing
all the ways the weight of weightlessness can heavy
down a dream or dream a story out of time.

OK So Mind Palaces Are Cool And All, But

on the laptop screen Jonny Lee Miller says he shot up because the world was too loud and my spouse looks over and I am only stimming a little bit / hardly flapping at all really / not even barely moving my hands enough to be alarming to anyone / and I say no that wasn't it / that wasn't it at all and I am only lying a little bit / hardly at all really / not even barely enough to count as false / it's not even white / not even that much of a harmless that it could count or weigh or cook up and leave something scorched and our fan whines just far enough below a C to burn / and the couch whispers against the back of my left leg / and lately when I've been more manic / like the last time I shot up / before we even kissed / I've taken again to listening to rain sounds exactly as loud as my speakers will make them / and that's not silence / it's not silence / so it can't be about too loud

can it?

I almost feel like if it were, sobriety would be a soft whisper in a mosh pit the way the world is just screaming all the time / I mean touch really is a kind of screaming / and Jonny Lee Miller is saying he's learned to quiet his mind / learned to build himself a place he can live / a palace he calls it / says he wanders the rooms and he finds the quiet / and good for him / good for him and his weird hands / he has such weird hands, they're always screaming, but some of us -

Tiara After a Year on HRT

I. Yes

hymn (the homonym expected,
expected meaning the turn to story,
turn also meaning transition,
transition too easy an expectation,
the expectation a story in itself,
to meaning always in progress,
to also meaning infinitive,
the unachievable, the repetition,
the meaning alone, singular,
meaning suggesting a logic,
hymn meaning song, meaning worship,
the opening of a mouth,
  also meaning both, and
  turn also meaning an ending)

II. Turn

also (meaning an ending,
the story turned
over in a casket,
over also meaning above,
also meaning the sky
and the earth were lovers, once,
turned meaning undead,
spell meaning to assemble,
to take the pieces of a tongue,
meaning to noise, to sound,
sound meaning able to symbol,
to weight with meaning,
  weight meaning to lower
  as one might into the earth

III. As

one (meaning the earth,
the casket, the lowering,
weight meaning memory,
memory meaning duty,
meaning fides, meaning proof,
meaning reason, meaning I am,
that meaning singular,
I meaning first / person meaning one,
meaning alone, meaning simile
like the sky, like meaning,
meaning comparison, using,
or meaning separation, meaning
  suggesting loss, suggesting grief,
  suggesting process, suggesting

IV. Suggesting

process (suggesting
a linear progression, a work
that can be completed, an extinction,
not an unclosed bracket,
not an incomplete god,
not an unfinished proof, qed
work = a body, qed
a line = an extinction, qed
to prove = to die, suggesting
meaning embodies work, suggesting
to body meaning to move with force,
often to accompany up, suggesting
  sky, the afterlife, clouds, rain,
    tears, oceans, bodies of water)

V. Tears

oceans (bodies of water,
suggesting tautology, suggesting
we contain oceans meaning tides
meaning the moon meaning the night
pulls all of us meaning we recede
and return, recede suggesting
retreat, suggesting fear, suggesting
the possibility of loss, possibility
meaning nothing is certain, nothing
meaning nothing meaning nothing is
meaning, is meaning ich meaning
the sound that catches in our throats
  meaning the cough meaning the hidden
  sob meaning drowning in oneself)

VI. Sob

meaning (drowning oneself
in symbols, suggesting signs,
suggesting sounds, suggesting
strait, sea, scent of salt, set
of sails, set suggesting still,
still suggesting stalled, stall
suggesting sale, cent, a stolen
sigh, a steel, a sonder, stranger
settling in sight, in scent,
in center, centered suggesting
sent, circling, searching, seek
suggesting find meaning
  the unexpected, the blank space,
  the mapless, the dragon)

VII. Map

Lest the dragon find the scent.
Lest the sails stall, the sky's
breath failing. Less the unexpected,
more the earth. More the work.
More the weight. More the tongued
ring of sibilance, the spell,
the ocean exhaling a lungful
of moon. More a song. More
a logic of failure. Lest the proof
succeed. Lest the mouths close,
the circles flatten into extinction,
into a tide of hymns. Suggesting
  certainty, setless, unsettled,
   unsingular, unexpected, unclosed

VIII. Unsingular

him (the hollow name expected,
the expectation a story in itself,
also meaning an ending,
also meaning the sky) -
one meaning: the earth
(meaning feelings, meaning proof,
process suggesting
not an incomplete god, but
oceans). bodies of water
pull all of us, meaning we recede,
meaning down in oneself
are sails. we set suggestions. still -
  let it drag on. fine. assent.
  more than weight. more the tongue.

still life with depressive episode

It takes me an hour today to escape bed,
though there is nothing pleasant holding me.
Though there is no holding. Though here
in this half-lit room, the shades draw
a half-shadow across every surface.
By the time I move, my hips are full

of slow and still stories, the quiet air full
of my breath. When I fold the bedsheets
behind me, reach the unbroken surface
of morning like some lake pulling me
from the shore, when I rise and draw
the shades, when I finally hear

the daybreak let out its breath. When here
becomes a following, a friend, a foal
stumbling after the night, tongue raw
from old and unexpected teeth, broad
weight precarious in the lean, the mien
of it a weighted average, some surfaces

carried more than others - but. Surfaces

always reflect the light. What there is. Here
the light is a whisper.

Winona Ryder says the dead man's name

three times, the world erupts
into a riot of color, crass
laughter and transformations
dancing across the screen,
and when everything calms
nothing is calm, or the same
shape it was before the shades
were drawn across the screen.
I've been writing more
in complicated tenses
these long and dour days. Would
have beens and could perhaps
have been fallings have
insisted on wandering into
my lines and making a bed
of me. I miss a simple present
when I let myself binge
on melancholy. To touch
seems to contain an infinitive
sense, to promise a summons
of a dead future. Again
a dead future. When the sky

turned a swirling bright
and the family, always
the family, considering how
to regather the missing. Another
infinitive, the looping back,
the arm and the arm and the arm
wrapped around a back
after the battle. The settle
set against a backdrop
of flashing devastation. Probably
there was a sorting, lambs
from lamplight, love from
whatever does not sound
like love. Certainly there was
conflict. We all know the dead
do not take kindly to those
who still live choosing when
the world should be emptied.
But what would it look like,
living kindly with the dead?
How could we even imagine
such strangeness, such quiet?

We sit in quiet and solitude

beneath a bridge. Something
meant to cross a current.
To hold bodies between metal
and water. I hold
a flame in my palm. His hand
gathers my waist. He asks
what I am afraid of. I say
I fear fire. When I was a small child,
a small room with a metal door
glowed open. Now, I do not door,
do not live in small rooms, do not trust
anything open or glowing. I watch
his eyes. The lashes. The weight
of speech. He crosses his legs
and leans back. His thighs are
a kind of water. A current.
For a moment, my throat could be
a net. A weave to catch something
falling. A search. A passive hunt.
A holding back. A barrier. Yesterday,
in a dream, I tell a story to a room
overflowing with eyes. My voice

paints the walls the color of steam.
The walls wrap all of us in current.
Carry us into breath until our lungs
forget the taste of city. Of burning.
of any way we knew to make the world
forget itself. The story has no weight.
Bears on nothing. What matters is
the prism of smoke it carries
from my throat. The ache to run.
To hide anywhere that would hold me.
I've never yet heard a city say it ached,
though certainly some hunger.
In the dream, I stare at a city's thighs
in a room full of smoke. I try to catch
desire when it falls from a bridge.
To find a hunt the current flows through.
My eyes choke on a tide of doors.
In the dream, I tell a story to myself.

Mulberry

Today, a friend asks how I am doing.
I wave my arms wildly at everything
and say considering, you know, not bad.

That's a small lie. The waving is restrained.
I am told that false harbors, lain outwards
from beaches on the north coast of France,

smoothed waters so men could walk
across them. The analogy of faith
is not lost on me - how sometimes

even distant storms must be worked away
before the waters can be trusted.
Even then, I am told, many drowned.

Not bad, I say. You know - I have harbors.
I shrug my eyes gently at everything.
Another small lie. When I can, I avoid

looking at everything. Too many. Too loud.
I am told the stories of beeswax

and binding are artifacts of translation.

That the danger was not the sound
but the seeing, or, really, any entrance
of desire into the flesh. I am told hunger

is a human universal, so Ii stop up
my eyes with feathers, choose to see
only the adornment of hollow bones.

A small lie, I say. Stillness. You know.
Considering everything's wildness.
The way a sudden storm left the false harbors

waving wildly until they had to be abandoned.
I am told the myth is of blood soaking
into the roots - of impatience, unwillingness

to wait past frost. The analogy about hunger
is not lost on me - how sometimes
safety requires a temporary starving.

Requires binding to the mast. Until
the ships sink. Until the waters still.
Until the singing fades into the sun.

I wouldn't call it hunger

After Imani Davis

I wouldn't call it hunger, what opens my mouth
when the doctor asks me if I have
any concerns. Not hunger exactly. More like
the feeling of a broken tooth
that has been worn into an almost-rhyme
in the back of my mouth.

More like that. More like my tongue
keeps coming back to it
every time I'm not talking.
More like a reunion. And the doctor
is very sweet. Asks how long
I have felt this way. What I know
about side effects, if the broken
might not be better than the blood.

I tell her I'm not broken, I've just tired
of navigating around my own sharp edges.
My hand follows the rough line of my jaw.

The teeth rasp against my skin.

I wouldn't call it a list exactly, what I call back
from my memory. More like a summoning.
More like a summons. A sigh. A siren. More like
a litany of what can go wrong
that I fear less than stasis. The doctor listens.
It is not odd to be grateful to be heard.
It is not odd to speak of hunger
when I am so full already.

I wouldn't call it joy, what curls my mouth.
Not joy, exactly. More like the first drink of water
after a long run, the cool and quiet
and nothing sharp or broken
to run my tongue against.
More like that.

Impact

Later, my lover
would say I can't
believe you didn't
tell me and I
would say I just
forgot, it wasn't
that big a deal
and I would be
telling the truth or
at least a truth or
at least the truth
for every moment
except the moments
it was a lie.

I was crossing the street
and - you know
the rest. The white
man in the car.
The honest thought
he's going to stop,
right? The hood.

The tumble. The stagger.
The word we use
to describe a need
for excision, a tooth
retreating into the comfort
of flesh. The reminder
that things give
at different rates.

How the mouth swells
around something harsh
that should know its place
and the places
it should avoid.
Gumline. Crosswalk.
Memory. I can believe
I forgot it. I can believe
so many forgettings.
I can forget so many
painful and solid things.

so here's the sky. i guess it's a gift.

or something like. let's go with yes.
let's close our hands around it. together.
do you feel the cool? the dry? how the wind
whorls your skin open the more you try
to hold it steady? how the vise of your fingers
helps the light elude them? but. this sky.
this particular arrangement of clouds
and emptiness. i give it to you. walk into it.
step carefully. the sky has never loved us
or anyone like us. how angry it must be
to be formed into a metaphor, asked
for permission, given. to give the sky,
i think, one must have watched a crick
for hours. must know the foam. must know
the flow of things, the way eddies leave
the leesides of stones smoothed and alone
and practically untouched except in
their sharpest insights. must know cliffs
and how the currents flow around them.
how, my love, there is a space of calm air
just beyond the point where anyone,
walking, would fall forever. let's go with yes.

let's open the dam and let the valley flood
with clouds. let's not hold too tight
to the trees looming skeletal against the sky
we've already woven into our wrists.
here: you can wear this breeze like a shawl.
the ends are already fraying against
the weight of our invocations. if you follow
the threads, you will find an endless supply
of breath. i hope you can take it in
the spirit we intended.

II

Anointed

No, it was more quiet than that. No torches,
just knowing we were the observant
children, the ones loved and loving
properly. We were the proper ones.
Upright. Libel-less our witness,
our sacred texts ours and no one else's.
We. Family, body, bride, groomed
from birth to love wholly and hate
temptation. Quieter than that. Prepared
for seduction by anything bright.
To be wary of anything dark or hooked
but a shepherd's staff. Any outsider
tongue or eye, the self formed from clay
and sacrifice. The future practically
burning honey in our mouths. We knew
the path, the practice, the foe, the whereof
and the unspoken. Quieter than that.
The choice to remain was easy
until it became a choice. Until the words
offered themselves up like laughter
or the ram. When the gates burst
and we stumbled blinking from the bright

city into all the Earth and all its choice.
It's frightening not to know the way.
To walk through every Earthly city
remembering every narrow, obvious path
and all that every path promised,
every easy enemy and light hearted
dismissal. To be told they tried to kill
the only one who'll ever love you,
or could, or should, there was a kind
of comfort there, in that sackcloth
and broken bowl, that scraping
and bowing to nothing but a father,
and no spirit's voice commanding
anything but obedience, anything
but the sword and the gnawing in the gut
and the closed eyes and the kneeling.

Listening, Florida, 1993

and my nana set the needle down
with careful hands, fitted it exquisitely
into the groove, and we all listened
to Tchaikovsky, sat on the floor
with crossed legs and closed eyes
and let the piano concerto wash
across our upturned throats so loud
our voices disappeared. Her hearing
was still good in those days, I think,
though I think her lungs had begun
already remembering too many places
she'd survived and left, but her ears
caught everything, and I can still
almost touch the way she translated
what she caught into a cackling,
and I can still see her laughter, lost
in the thundering keys, when the great
cadenza startled my eyes and throat
and the whole good world open
into shaking, and I can almost
remember her voice.

Will

Say the ground splits open and swallows
a house. The trees ringing the property

will still pull water from the earth. They
will not ask what happened in the house,

if the family that lived there was a happy one,
or if the family was swallowed by the earth.

They will, perhaps, ask after the salt
levels of the water. They will, perhaps,

ask if the thing they pull into themselves
more closely resembles a glacier,

or sadness, or, perhaps, joy.
To be clear, the earth was not hungry.

It devoured carelessly, thoughtlessly,
paying no mind to its devouring.

To be clear, the trees did not thirst.

Though they drank, and drink, and will

drink until the earth is a wasteland,
there is no will to them. A will is a curious

document, evidence of life, but not of living.
To be clear, a glacier has no will,

though it leaves behind a new world,
an inheritance, though it makes

and remakes its way with a thousand
numb hands. To be cold

is to lose your way. To be swallowed
by the earth is to find your way laid out

for you. Not to will, but to leave behind
a new and gasping land.

Void

on the way to work, I catch myself sobbing
for the loneliness of a fictional God.
The god of my father, the phrase goes.

Father, son, the whole Trinity and still
alone. These days, when I wonder if
the plague will catch me, I think often of immortality.

How never leaving means there will be
no one to remember you. A neat
trap. Inescapable. The only way out,

I tell myself, is - I wonder if this fictive
everything can change. The mind. If.
They must have gone mad, then.

The forever when before meant nothing.
When they made time and it, too, left them.

With

and all the all that set itself against
and then the all that set itself selftowards
and then the sun and some that did not set
unwalked on tired legs away away

and when the whens were wandered off
and all the alls were set whichever
and everything and everything else
togethering finally with full arms

then the witching with the lovely was
and all the everythings togethered bright
and all the ifs becoming sums and suns
unsetting in their setless and

and all the ands and all the all all were
and lovelied bright becomings whomed and thered
and there the then thenned selfed and full
and all the was was withed, and is

What my parents called me

First:
   pride

Then:
   disappointment

Then:

Garden

To say it started with fire
would be far too dramatic. Try
it started when we looked back. Say
we saw the sword, the hand, the state
of the world awaiting us, thick plait
of rivers woven across the desert's back,
and we stood by the doorway and talked
about the days before we'd fallen.
There was enough blame to fallow
any field. I can't remember if we knew
what burning was, before the law.
If we knew how to till ash before the toll,
how to fold the fallen into dirt and fool
the furrowed brow of earth into filling
itself with soft and green and tall, tilled,
tale-bearing children. We can call this
one, we said. Surely he'll answer. Here's
another, and isn't it lovely how tender
brothers tending? How kindness and care
build worlds together for play, cure
all the gardens we'd given over to the curse?

Lamech, by the forge

After, my son began making
swords. While he hammered
and heated, I listened to the iron
cry out. The bow was always
a better friend. How the arrows
flew away like my wives did,
but fetched me bloody and fatty
and tasteful things, enough
to skewer and burn. All good
meat's a proper sacrifice.
A good and righteous death.
We'll buy off the eternal.
We've known that long enough.
They never see the arrow.

My son says he'll walk me
to the field tonight. Says
I can have one more hunt.
In the dark, it don't matter
how old my eyes are. My hands
are still strong. Sometimes
I bring them together just so

and all the birds fall from the sky,
their wings wearing bones
like feathers. My bow and I,
we used to be kinder.
Aging makes us all cruel,
my son says to comfort me.

He's a good child. Strong.
Gentle with his blades.
I raised him well. Tomorrow
I'll tell him. Today I'll listen
to his good work and look
forward to the killing. He's
a namesake, a seventh son.
I hear the old man's around
somewhere. He always was
a wanderer, the old man. Ha.
Look at me, repeating myself.
Ah, well. I'll allow myself some
repetition. A little wobble
in the flight, some loose feathers.
Not the worst thing to repeat,
a word sometimes. Wander,
that's a good one. I like family,
too. I made a good one.
A strong line. My hand in his,
we'll walk safe and straight
as any bowstring.

Diluvian

Sometime after the beginning, we built,
and before done building, we boarded
and said we'd boarded well, and wrested
nights from the feel of fear to drown
the whole world, and when we worked
we worked well together, warped the boards
to fit around a frame as we always had
but more. It's a dreadful thing
to have so large a purpose. To wash wood
with pitch and pitch yourself against the drowning
the divine's allowed. Sometime after,
a man will speak of thread and fire and mercy
and a room will gasp for breath and their eyes
will be a thousand Earths the way I know this Earth
and a different we will say the room awakened,
will allow the allbefore was only ever dream
or dreamless sleep, will wallow in a world
washed clean. I can't help but wonder
why they're still drawn to water. When I opened
and lay down on Ararat, I swore I'd never touch
the stuff again. Better the wine. Better
the crushed, the changed and changing,

the stained lips and deepest sleep,
better anything so staggering
it washes everything away.

Laughter

Such an absurd little creature,
  little brother, half-
     walking, barely off

  milk and I looking over him,
    squatting and souring in the dust,
hardly a symbolic threat, and I

have kept covenant, been good,
  a good son, first and only
arrow in my father's quiver, his pride

for fourteen years
  sated - he was already old
when I was born, he was so happy

my mother said - she said he was happy
to have me. It's practically a joke
  this business of promises, names,

  gods, what I would do
    to be loved by them.

He promised me - I'm the son, the promise

his wife made - me, her firstborn
   if you think about it the right way -
  my mother did as she was told. So do I

  want, and want, and keep
a straight face, do I never look up
 at my father's

lands? Down at this little whelp
  placed into my keeping, my
hold, me, the good steward

  of that which will
dispossess me? I - hear
my father call. I can't leave

 the boy alone,
can I? I promised
I'd watch him until his mother

  came back. I promised -
 I was promised - I am
  a good son -

Burning

after Torrin Greathouse

Once, my mother said she saw a demon
curled inside my chest. Once, my lover's face
was a waning moon, then a crescent,
then new, and then the night was blindingly
full of stars, half of them already dead
but the light still enough to see by.
When I was young, I burned my hands
on a wood stove, and my mother
wrapped them in gauze. Once, my lover
traced the scars crawling from my fingers
to my wrists, the clumsy places where I had healed
half curled, and clawed, and crescent.
You can barely tell, he said, they'll be gone soon.
Once, my lover mistook himself
for my scars, for something I'd survive.
He was right. When I was taken home,
my mother locked me in a small room.
Withdrawal is a kind of exorcism,
the way everything hiding within your flesh
becomes suddenly obvious.

When he overdosed, I began to understand fire,
how there is something wild
living inside anything that will burn,
just waiting to hiss and sizzle
and smoke the stars out.

A funny thing

about losing

your family:

you're always

a little afraid

they'll come back.

The Theft of Fire

if life is the slow burn of loss / then forgive me //
for keeping a few extra matches / in my pocket.
- Brandon Melendez

We all want the warm, I think. When the sun
sinks away from us, we all huddle around
its memory and tell ourselves it's not forever.
Forgive me this universalizing, and its necessary

blindness. The legend is that someone needed to suffer
so we could blind ourselves to the dark. So the night's
teeth would fear us. I mean, the gift wasn't the flame,
it was the control. Not the burn, but the chance

to slow its spread. To hold it still. To hold the hurt
and know it will only sometimes make us into itself.
Forgive me: Sometimes the scars drown out the good
the flame can carry. Sometimes flesh remakes itself

like water swallowing stones, but sometimes
it prefers to become a clay field, furrowed
from the plowshare. I mean, another legend says

the gift was meant to make the iron soft enough

to shape, the warmth a side effect, but, the moral
is still the suffering. The beating of nature into
a new form. The punishment lasting forever. I mean only
that the lake of fire still means the world to me. Forgive me:

I mean its end. I don't mean to boast of these small
epiphanies. Only to understand the way the sky opens
when the smoke thins, or how a dying fire still gives off
enough heat to pull away from, or hold close.

Poem in which the fire refuses to be a metaphor

The fire declines to represent love,
or lust, or the loss of anything
so flammable as emotion.

The fire finds a substance that will burn,
and the fire does not seek
in the ways that hands seek.

The fire does not search
for an entrance as eyes do.
Does not grasp or gasp as skin does.

The fire refuses to stand in
for any kind of hunger.
Gives the evening to

the mouth, the play of wet tongue
and crooked teeth, and the fire
knows how both char, but

the fire refuses to carry
the scent. The fire leaves

that weight for the air,

the moving air, heavy with ash
and memory, the air that creates
a coastline in each eddy,

the air that carves momentary
countries from flakes of gray like snow
falling into an innocent sky.

The fire could almost weep
it's all so beautiful, how these thin
creatures that are not

the ghosts of trees, and are not birds,
and are not prayers
or anything else with wings

still float upward -

Haiku

Tree (and of course a tree
is always a family, always burying,
hungering, connected to the earth)
      closes arms (and somehow we
always personify a tree)
             tight

against (and here we might see
the connection to closes, the sense
of a door that is no longer a door)
      the unquilting (the homely
made unhomelike, always uncanny)
                  clouds,

the wind, (or, the movement away)
      the cold rain.

Sonnet

on a theme by Edwin Morgan

a boy / a child / a voice /   if once a boy /
a sound / a sounding bell   across a lake /
a tone / atone / atonal /   listened / poised
atomic / atomized / all   gray and grace
apart / a part / a port   ion / charged by less /
apportioned / almost a beat /   almost / less
a break / abreast / a form /   across / a cross /
a crossing / ache / a rose /   arising / crest
a rise / a rib / a riddance /   waved and trod
a ride / a right / alright /   arid sand
a dam / a damn / a dance   and fall / and crawl
a hand / a height / a haunt /   away / always
  a hunt / a help / a hilt   away / and home
  away / a way / a will   away / and gone

Contrapuntal

Zeno's paradox suggests
                an arrow can never arrive -
you can never actually
                become anything - try to
exit a closet -
                catch even a molecule of air -
when you try - each step
                disasters across the floor -
vanishes into the smallness
                every child knows -
under the bed -
                fletched or fledgling - any feathered thing
twisting shadow through the slats -
                growing hungry for impact
soon - the silence
                has swallowed an empty room -
ravels in the voice -
                in this version of arrival the arrow never stops
quieting - the quaver
                justifying its loneliness -
promising no - no -
                knowing the story is of the air

over and over again -

        listening for someone who

never

        made it to the finish

III

Pantoum

I call a prayer out of every night
my dreams erase. I build an altar from
geometries; I worship patterns, fall
or follow sequences until I home

my dreams in space. I build, I alter, form
my heart in hollow, halt or halter, hope
the fallow sequences can till, can hone,
can stretch a structured silence into sleep.

My heart's allowed to halt, to falter, cope
with falling, break, or beak, or feathered wing
to stretch conjectures mindful back to reap
a field's untidy leavings. Gentle, this:

the oddities, untidy patterns, the slow
unmaking of every prayer I've told myself.

When I wake, my roommate has brewed coffee

and this is love: to know the moment
of another's rising and render from heat
the arms that will hold them until
they can hold themself. The coffee

is a bridge: I say this in the kindest sense,
a way across a river, a walk into the day,
a span, a spin of milk and sweet and gentle
acid, an aside in an empty theatre. To play

honestly. To open is to begin, or, to end
the process of making. I kiss him
on the forehead. I say thank you when
my cup is empty. If there were enough time.

When I leave, my roommate turns the coffee
off. It would char, he says, and goes to sleep.

Towards a definition of use value

1. In the provided space, write your truth.
Use a pencil.

2. Erase your answer from step 1.
Write the thing you actually wanted to say.

3. Erase your answer from step 2.
Write the thing you didn't want to say.

4. Between the letters of your answer from step 3,
write the detail your coping mechanisms strangled

before it began to breathe, then the detail
still blast-proofing its blank-walled sanctuary.

5. Study the way in which your truths are woven.
Shadow the provided space with your shaking.

6. Don't be afraid. Is all of this so very unnatural?
Breathe. Let it catch in your throat. Breathe.

1. Money has three functions. In barter economies,
living things often serve as stores of value.

2. I needed a safe space. He offered. Whenever you need.
It was a Thursday afternoon, so I waited in the hallway.

3. I had already defined "safe space." It meant: not home.
Definitions are important. They let you control reality.

4. My shirt scabbed to my back until he pulled it off me.
I staggered after the first beer, but kept cracking pull-tabs

to be a better store of value. I kissed him first.
My spine shook like a medicine cabinet.

5. He put his clothes on. He said he wasn't gay.
His voice shook. I fell asleep leaving fingerprints on him.

6. He kept breathing. I spiraled in the space between
his back and the wall. Something caught in my throat.

Salt

My spouse mentions that I speak of my parents
in the past tense. I hear something about salt,

something about every word I have swallowed
that does not love me in the way the ocean does,

does not wrap me in a thousand arms and pull me close.
I write a poem inspired by the way I have lost them,

though they are still living, somewhere, so far as I know.
I say the poem is "in conversation" with this Death Cab song

I used to listen to when I wanted to hold loss close
without letting it fill my lungs. I write a poem "after" a singer

who drowned, and his songs are not dead, do not sit
quietly on the page, but do not hold me, do not speak

in the present tense, do not taste of salt
or anything else the ocean leaves behind.

I refuse to write a poem about grief,
or about death, or in conversation

with death. I refuse to continue
my conversation with any poem

that does not want to hold me. If
I must call grief an empty shore to rob

its arms of their ability to grasp, then
so be it. I have been tired for too many years

of letting grief claim its territory uncontested,
have seen living things turn slowly to sand

too many times. If I want to follow a cycle
of tides without thinking of the dead,

who will call me jealous? Who will say
I owe the ocean more than I owe the living?

My spouse mentions
I speak of my parents
in the past tense.
I imagine sometimes

my parents speak of me
the same way.
I imagine sometimes
my parents speak of me.

That they remember me
and salt
creeps into the roots
of their tongues

and keeps anything
from growing -

That damn quilt

she says, and she is almost my friend,
but is not, and will not be, though owing
nothing to this conversation. The quilt
is still new to me, young as I am

in the fresh, surprising cold of our debate.
She is not young. She has found her way
here after seeing many stitched-together
things consumed by flight and dust

and the desire for a home. It's an act
of grieving, she says, of course, but, also
there's a limit to the politics of visibility.
I nod and say sometimes being seen

  means making yourself, and sometimes
  it only means making yourself a target.

We talk about transformations
through her Merlot and my cheap bourbon
until I can almost forget the weight of my owing
to the old, dead or otherwise, to those

who made themselves, seen or otherwise,
or otherwise wove the names together
into something that could keep a body warm.
I wove my grief, once, saw the loom of it,

followed the thick tough thread of each
I had lost until I reached a knotted place.
I do not carry my dead on my skin. I do
consider myself not a tapestry. Patchwork,

  perhaps, some doll some boy's father
  will tell him not to hold close.

My almost friend gets up to leave
and I say thank you
thank you for bringing me here
and she leaves before I can avoid

my own question. I watch her walk
down a street full of children.
I say I don't think I meant
a place. Sometimes it is so impossible

to here that I forget to yesterday,
so definitive to now
that I forget to quilt
or cold or cut the thread

  when the stitch
  is done.

I have never been good
at letting my dead stay dead.

I have enough, any muse
might think, to sharp

the squares together.
Enough to cover anything

that should be warm.
Enough to be the old one

complaining about a quilt.
Sometimes I am. Sometimes

I wish to be seen, or to forget
the weight but remember

the warm. I home. I pull
a nameless quilt across my chest.

There's this story I tell myself

that joy is a bird
who has been imprisoned
in a cage of bones

that the bird finally
shreds its wings
against the bars

that joy crawls bleeding
between the bones
and into a forest

that each tree there
is made of bone
and whispers run

  that the bird listens
  and nests anyway -

There's this story I tell myself

that I am made of birds, or joy, or
I swallowed a cage once, and now
there is a tree of iron feathers
taking root in my throat -

that my throat is a forest, or a home, or
I carved out my skeleton once, and now
everything is soft
and I do not know whether to be afraid -

that my fear is wingless, or bloody, or
I opened a door once, and now
there are feathers everywhere
and I do not know if the bird is still alive -

and I do not know if the forest is still whispering -
and I do not know if I should listen -

There's this story I tell myself

about joy, I mean, a bird, how it flies, I mean,
crawls, bleeding, out of flesh, I mean,
a cage, I mean,

about a cage that bleeds, I mean,
opens up, and something bloody, I mean,
wingless, crawls into a forest, I mean,

about escaping a cage, I mean,
the past, how it builds, I mean, nests,
in our bones, I mean, the trees, I mean,

about the way our skeletons, I mean,
memories, root themselves in us, I mean,
the past, how they whisper to us run

and we listen
and nest anyway

There's this story I tell myself

about how much one thing
can look like another -
that joy can look like some animal -

that a forest can look like a cage -
that the difference
between a bird and a cage is

that one has hollow bones
and the other
is a hollow thing -

that the difference
between a cage and a forest is
that the bird chose one -

that the bird crawled into it
and called it its own -

There's this story I tell myself

the concept is
that having a body
can be bearable

that I am beginning to accept,
if not birds,
at least an idea of feathers

that when I listen to my bones
I still want to run away
or shred myself against them, but

that when I examine my pulse
closely enough
I do not hear a cage

  and I see nothing bloody
  that should not be.

About the Author

Michael Hodges teaches and writes in Seattle, Washington. They are a two-time Rain City Poetry Slam Hoodie Slam winner and have represented Rain City at the National Poetry Slam and Individual World Poetry Slam.

Originally from the South, they have also lived in Pittsburgh, where they taught at Winchester Thurston School and were a member of the 2018 Steel City Slam NPS team.

Their work has appeared in *Drunken Boat*, *Magma*, *The Santa Ana River Review*, the anthology *In the Shadow of the Mic* (Bridge and Tunnel Books), and elsewhere.

Acknowledgments

To everyone who helped make this book happen.

CPSIA information can be obtained
at www.ICGtesting.com
Printed in the USA
BVHW090126100422
633823BV00007B/71

9 781942 547167